An Egg Is Quiet

Black-necked Stilt

Green Vegetable Bug

Steller's Jay

Snow Bunting

Northern Shrike

Blue Crab

Lobster

Prothonotary Warbler

Arctic Tern

Black-capped Mockingthrush

Brewer's Sparrow

Field Cricket

Blue Joy

Fork-tailed Storm-petrel

Elegant Tinamou

Bronze-winged Jacana

Streaked Bit

Hawfinch

California Thrasher

Anna's Hummingbird

Yellow-billed Cuckoo

Long-tailed Tailorbird

Common Murre

Turkey

Booted War

Green Lacewing

Atlantic Salmon

Red-winged Blackbird

Chipping Sparrow

Glossy Ibis

Ladybird Beetle

Golden-crowned Kinglet

Paradise Crow

Cactus Wren

Boat-tailed Grackle

Scarlet Tanager

Leopard Frog

Herring Gull

Townsend's Solitaire

Hepatic Tanager

Harlequin Bug

Evening Grosbeak

Kirtland's Warbler

Emperor Penguin

Passion Vine Butterfly

Black Vulture

Little Blue Heron

Dogfish

Chukar

Thick-billed Warbler

Paradise Riflebird

Gray Catbird

Sooty Tern

Yellowhammer

Bushy-crested Jay

American Robin

Green Iguana

Black-naped Oriole

Katydid

Black Swallowtail E.

To my mom, Candy Champion Hutts, who hatched me.
~D. A.

Welcome to the new hatchling in the Long family! Your
Nana Long loves you dearly and will enjoy watching you
discover the natural wonders of this world. ~S. L.

The author and illustrator wish to thank Frankie D. Jackson
and Dr. Jack Horner, Department of Earth Sciences,
Montana State University; Blake Newton, the University of Kentucky;
Pauline Tom, founder and president of the Texas Bluebird Society;
Martha Tacha, wildlife biologist; and Fred Bervoets.

ISBN-13: 978-0-545-05424-9
ISBN-10: 0-545-05424-9

12 11 10 9 8   14/0

Printed in the U.S.A.   40
First Scholastic Book Club printing, March 2009

Book design by Sara Gillingham
Handlettered by Anne Robin and Sylvia Long
The illustrations in this book were rendered
in ink and watercolor.

Black Swallowtail

An Egg Is Quiet

by Dianna Aston ~ illustrated by Sylvia Long

SCHOLASTIC INC.
New York   Toronto   London   Auckland   Sydney
Mexico City   New Delhi   Hong Kong   Buenos Aires

Black-necked Stilt

An egg is quiet.

It sits there, under its mother's feathers . . .

Anna's Hummingbird

on top of its father's feet . . .

Emperor Penguin

Kemp's Ridley Sea Turtle

buried beneath
the sand.

Warm. Cozy.

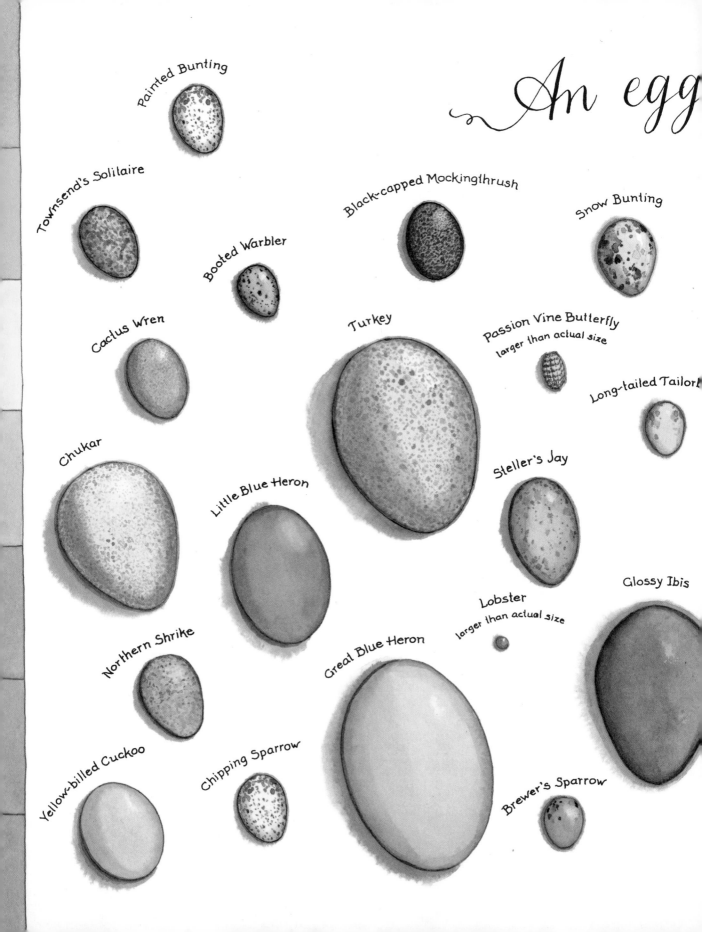

Painted Bunting

Townsend's Solitaire

Black-capped Mockingthrush

Snow Bunting

Booted Warbler

An egg

Cactus Wren

Turkey

Passion Vine Butterfly
larger than actual size

Long-tailed Tailor!

Chukar

Little Blue Heron

Steller's Jay

Glossy Ibis

Northern Shrike

Lobster
larger than actual size

Great Blue Heron

Yellow-billed Cuckoo

Chipping Sparrow

Brewer's Sparrow

...s colorful.

Fork-tailed Storm-petrel

...k-naped Oriole

Bushy-crested Jay

King Salmon

Prothonotary Warbler

Thick-billed Warbler

Blue Crab

Kirtland's Warbler

...reaked Bittern

Herring Gull

Golden-crowned Kinglet

Field Cricket

Blue Jay

Hawfinch

Elegant Tinamou

American Robin

California Thrasher

...patic Tanager

Gray Catbird

There are round eggs.

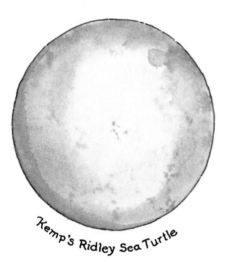

Kemp's Ridley Sea Turtle

Sea turtles dig a hole in the sand with their flippers and lay up to 200 soft, round eggs. Round eggs fit together nicely in tight spaces.

There are oval eggs.

Ladybird Beetle
larger than actual size

When ladybugs hatch as larvae, their first meal is often the egg case they crawled out of.

s shapely.

There are even tubular eggs.

There are pointy eggs.

Dogfish

Common Murre

While most sharks give birth
to live young, some sharks,
like the lesser-spotted dogfish, begin
life in a leathery egg case with
tendrils. The tendrils anchor the eggs
to seaweed so they won't be
swept away by the ocean current.

Seabird eggs are pointy at
one end, so if they're laid on rock
ledges, they roll around in
safe little circles, not off the cliff.

The markings on some eggs
help them blend in with their
surroundings. This is called *camouflage*.
Camouflage is an egg's way of hiding.

An egg

Sooty Tern

s clever.

An egg might be speckled to
resemble the rocks around it. Or it
might be gray, the color of mud by a lake.
An egg does not want to be eaten by
a raccoon or a snake or a fox or an insect.

1" 2" 3" 4" 5" 6" 7" 8"

Ostrich

An ostrich egg can weigh as much
as 8 pounds. It is so big and so round,
it takes two hands to hold one egg.

Eggs come in different sizes.

Anna's Hummingbird

Hummingbird eggs are the size of a jelly bean. It would take about 2,000 hummingbird eggs to equal the size of one ostrich egg.

Paradise Crow

Yellowhammer

Green Lacewing

Red-winged Blackbird

An egg

Atlantic Salmon

Scarlet Tanager

Bronze-winged Jacana

Paradise Riflebird

Arctic Tern

Evening Grosbeak

Sooty Tern

artistic.

Katydid

Harlequin Bug

There are hard eggs

Boat-tailed Grackle

Bird eggs are hard.

and soft eggs

Green Iguana

Reptile eggs are often soft and rubbery.

and gooey eggs.

Leopard Frog

Amphibian eggs are gooey. The "goo" keeps them from drying out.

s textured.

and rough eggs.

There are smooth eggs

Southern Cassowary

Black Vulture

The eggs of cassowaries, emus,
and cormorants are rough.

Most bird eggs are smooth.

An egg might even

The remains of creatures that died millions of years ago may become rock-hard, or *fossilized*. Scientists have unearthed fossilized dinosaur eggs all around the world. Some are round, and some are oblong. Some are as small as one inch across, and some are as large as twenty inches. Scientists believe all dinosaurs hatched from eggs.

e fossilized!

An egg is giving.

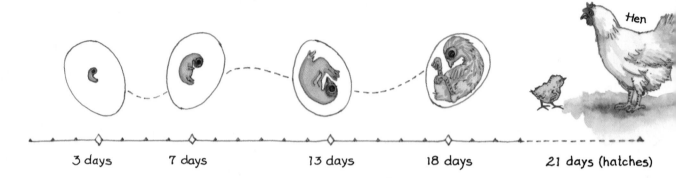

Hen

| 3 days | 7 days | 13 days | 18 days | 21 days (hatches) |

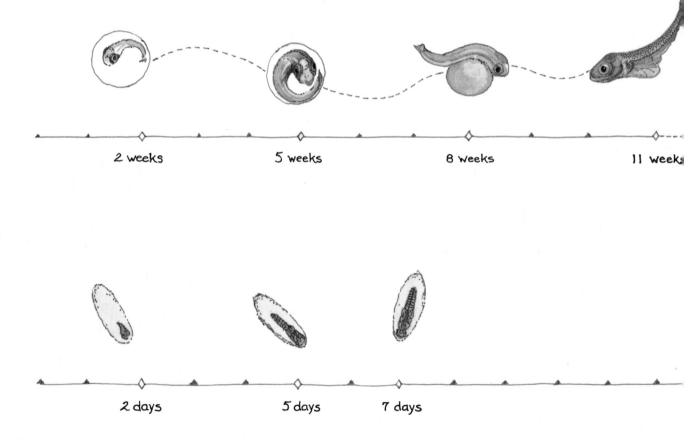

| 2 weeks | 5 weeks | 8 weeks | 11 weeks |

| 2 days | 5 days | 7 days |

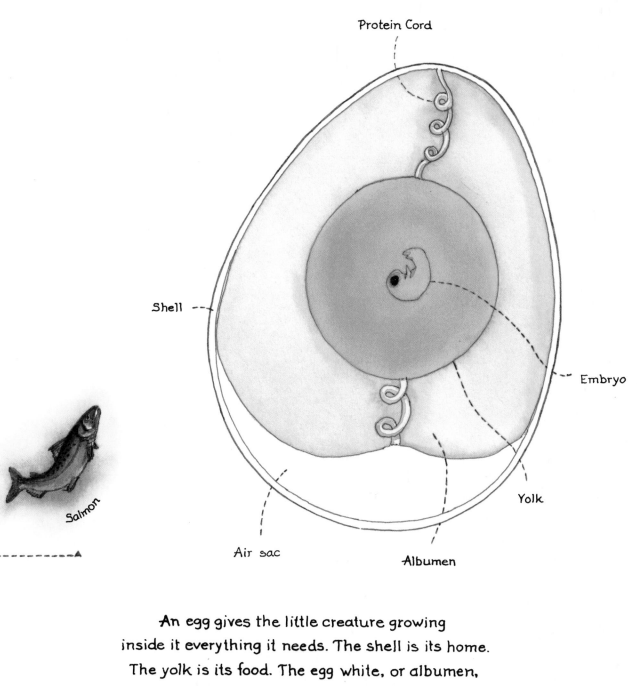

Protein Cord

Shell - -

Embryo - - -

Yolk

Air sac

Albumen

Salmon

An egg gives the little creature growing
inside it everything it needs. The shell is its home.
The yolk is its food. The egg white, or albumen,
is its pillow. The shell is covered with
teeny tiny holes, which allow air to enter.

Grasshopper

15 days

A grasshopper embryo rests inside the egg
until the weather is just right.

An egg is quiet

Then, suddenly . . .

Black-necked Stilt

Green Vegetable Bug

crunch!

an egg

cheep!

pe

Black-necked Stilt Nestlings

Paradise Riflebird

Passion Vine Butterfly

Steller's Jay

Lobster

Green Vegetable Bug

Fork-tailed Storm-petrel

Prothonotary Warbler

Elegant Tina

Snow Bunting

Common Murre

Bushy-crested Jay

Northern Shrike

Blue Crab

Arctic Tern

Streaked Bitter

Kirtland's Warbl

Herring Gull

California Thrasher

Boat-tailed Grackle

Emperor Penguin

Black Vulture

Katydid

Hawfinch

Cactus Wren

Yellowhammer

Blue Jay

Long-tailed Tailorbird

Harlequin Bug

Hepatic Tanager

Townsend's Solitaire

Chukar

Anna's Hummingbird

Atlantic Salmon

Leopard Frog

Black-capped Mockingthrush

Bronze-winged Jacana

Red-winged Blackbird

Paradise Crow

Glossy Ibis

Green Lacewing

Golden-crowned Kinglet

Scarlet Tanager

Yellow-billed Cuckoo

Turkey

Black-necked Stilt

Blue Heron

Thick-billed Warbler

Sooty Tern

Brewer's Sparrow

Booted Warbler

Chipping Sparrow

Evening Grosbeak

Gray Catbird

Black-naped Oriole

Field Cricket

Dogfish

American Robin

Ladybird Beetle

Green Iguana